This book was written to give children a little understanding of fish keeping along with the adventures of Fred The Fish. I am an avid fish keeper and have had numerous aquariums growing up. Currently I operate a maintenance aquarium business and have always enjoyed fishkeeping. The artist, an animator/illustrator, has many years of experience in the art field.

Author: Fred Freda
Illustrated by AnnMarie Freda

Addison,

Best Wishes

Fred the fish was born on a warm summers' day in the Sunshine State of Florida.

Fred was a clown fish which is a saltwater tropical fish. He was bright orange with white stripes and black on the end of his fins.

Fred would swim around in his large aquarium with the rest of his friends.

He would just play around all day. His favorite game was tag. He would chase his friends around and then his friends would chase him around.

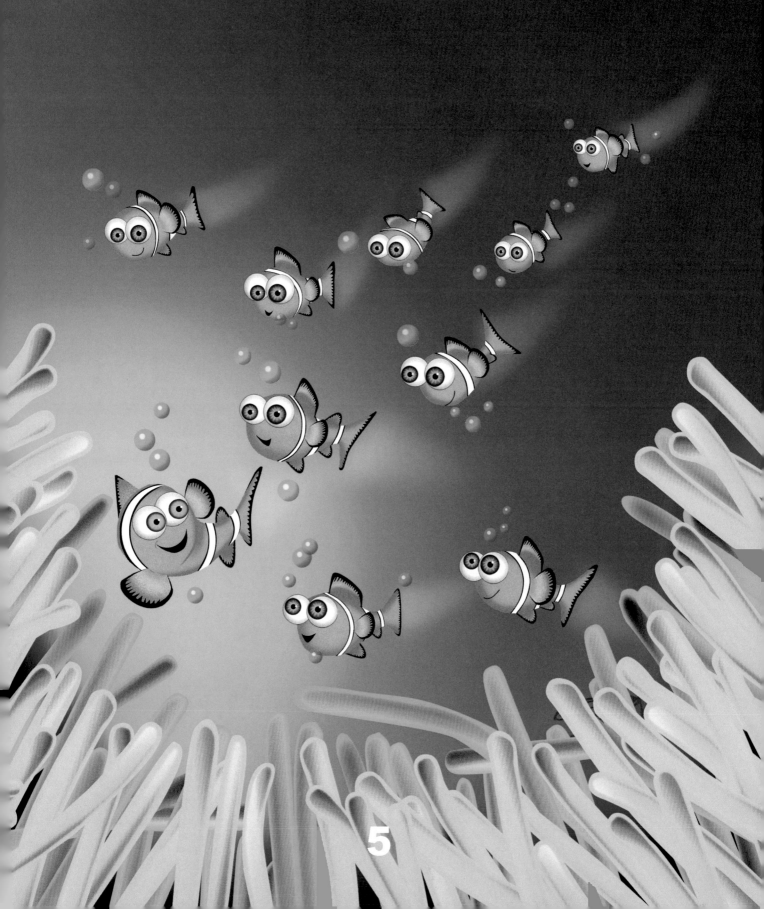

But Fred's favorite time of day was feeding time. A man that took care of Fred and his friends would come to their big aquarium and sprinkle fish flake food on the top of the water. The man was careful not to overfeed Fred and his friends.

Soon after eating all their food it began to get dark and the man would turn off the large light that hung over Fred's aquarium. Fred knew that this meant it was time for sleep.

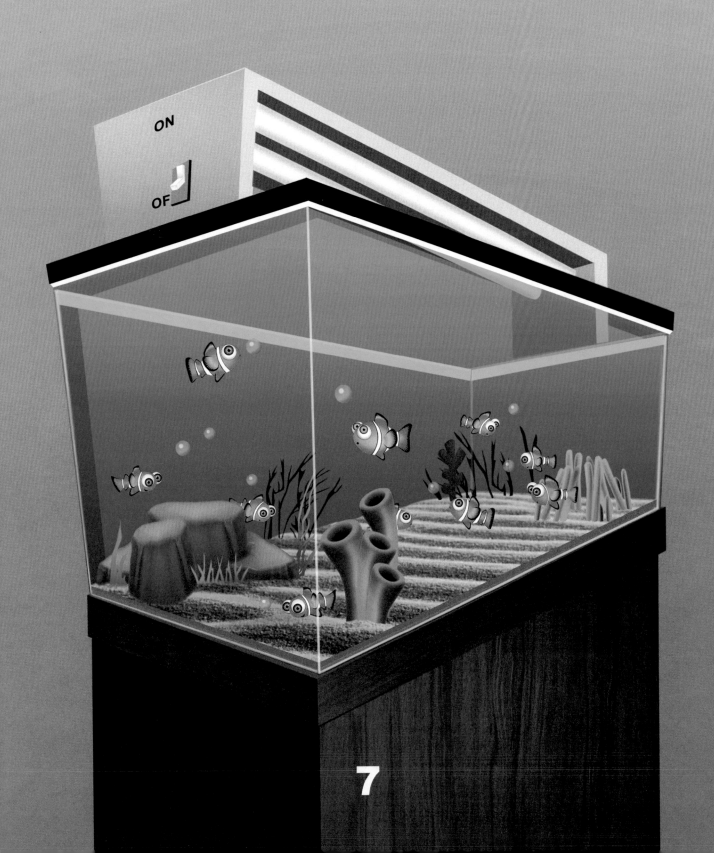

But unlike humans, Fred would fall asleep not in a bed, but by just floating very still in one place. Just a little wiggle here and there with his fins would keep him in the same place all night.

One day when Fred turned four weeks old, the man came with a large net and started to try to catch Fred and some of his friends.

Fred would swim fast as he could so the man couldn't catch him with the net. Fred was very scared and did not know what was happening.

Finally, Fred got too tired and was caught by the man's net. He was placed in a very large plastic bag with some of his friends. The man also put some air bubbles in the bag before closing it so they could breathe.

They were then put into a large box and sent to another place. It was dark and Fred was afraid.

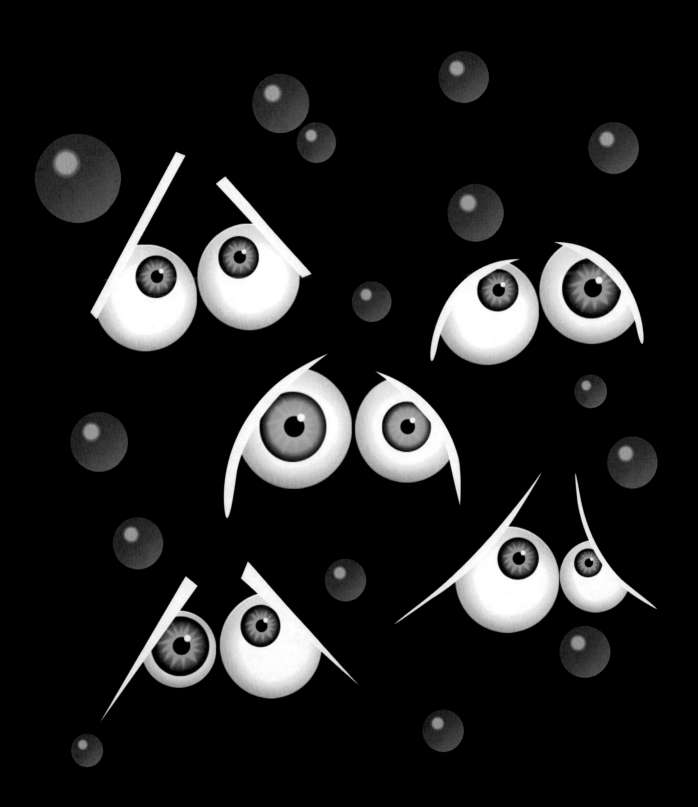

After a day, Fred and his friends arrived at their new home. Another man then opened the box that Fred was in and took the bag and placed it into another aquarium.

You see the temperature of the water in Fred's bag got cool during his trip. The man didn't want Fred to get sick so he let the water in the aquarium warm up the water in Fred's bag for few minutes. Then he let Fred out into his new aquarium.

Fred and his friends were happy again in their new home and once again started to play their favorite game of tag.

But Fred noticed that this place was different than where he was born. There were other types of fish in different aquariums around Fred's. Fred wondered why these fish were different than his friends and him.

Fred also wondered why children and their parents would come look in his aquarium as he played. Fred finally realized he was in a pet shop and these people were looking for fish to buy as pets.

17

One day the man came around and caught Fred and three of his friends with a net. He put them in a clear plastic bag with bubbles and gave them to a little boy to take to his house as pet fish.

Once the little boy was home he followed the instructions that the man from the pet shop gave him. Float the bag and make sure the water temperature was warm and then let Fred and his friends swim out into their aquarium.

Fred noticed that there were other fish in his new home that were different than his friends and him. Then he remembered the pet shop and recalled the other fish in the aquariums.

20

Soon they all became friends, playing tag and hide and seek. But still their favorite time was when the little boy sprinkled the fish food into the aquarium.

21

They all ate their share, remembering what the man at the pet shop said about giving them too much food to eat.

Fred grew up fast and loved his friends and especially the little boy who loved them too.

23

This book is being dedicated to all children who have pets. For each book sold a 30 cent donation will be given to the charity for cruelty to animals.

Made in the USA
Middletown, DE
17 February 2017